The Little Girl That Hides Inside of Me

Cynthia V. Avent

Diligence Publishing Company
Bloomfield, New Jersey

The Scripture in this book is from the King James Version and the New International Version.

**THE LITTLE GIRL THAT
HIDES INSIDE OF ME**

Copyright © 2020 Cynthia Avent
c/o Diligence Publishing Company
P.O. Box 2476
Bloomfield, New Jersey

All Rights Reserved

No part of this book may be reproduced in any form without the written permission from the publisher except for brief passages included in a review.

To contact Cynthia V. Avent speak at your church, organization, seminar or conference email: Cynthia's contact information:

**THE LITTLE GIRL THAT
HIDES INSIDE OF ME**

ISBN: 978-1-7374840-2-8

Printed in the United States

TABLE OF CONTENTS

Dedication 5
Chapter 1: The Silent Cry 7
Chapter 2: The Child Within 13
Chapter 3: Thirsty 17
Chapter 4: Broken For Freedom 21
Chapter 5: Born For Greatness 27
Chapter 6: What Is Trust? 29
Chapter 7: The Power of God Makes Us Free 33
About The Author 37
Order Information 39

DEDICATION

I dedicate this book to every young person who went through hard times, trials and tribulations in their life that made them feel stuck. Know that God has a great plan for your life and as you keep growing in God, He will heal the little boy or the little girl that lives or even hides inside of you.

I also dedicate this book to the three children that God has blessed me with, Atiyonna James, Keyonnah James and Zyion Miller.

Finally, I dedicate this book to everyone that helped me get this far in life.

CHAPTER 1

The Silent Cry

There are many people in this world that go through so much in life, but sometimes they don't know what to do. They don't know if they should scream or just let out a hard cry.

Sometimes people feel so much hurt in their lives and feel alone. They could be in a room full of people, but still feel lonely...like no one can hear them. So many children are victims of sexual abuse and carry the wounds of that abuse into their adulthood, living in the same desolate condition as Tamar in the Bible. Scripture simply tells us that she remained desolate in her brother's house. She was locked in the silence, shame, violation, and trauma of the abuse she suffered at the hands of her half-brother.

Christ promised healing for those who are hurt and wounded. Isaiah 61:1-3 beautifully describes the promise of transformation and healing through our Redeemer, Jesus Christ. God is beckoning us to accept His offer for healing, and to walk with one another along that journey of healing...out of the darkness and silence into His light with voices raised in hope and joy.

My story begins at the age of 10...when I lost my childhood...

I was born into a family of ten children, four girls and six boys. I was the seventh child. I can remember my father beating my mother many times when he was drunk. My mom would leave the house every night and wouldn't return until the next day, but she would always make sure there was food in the house. There are days she would go to bed hungry, but she always made sure that us children had something to eat.

When, I was ten years old, my cousin and her boyfriend moved in with us. My cousin would go out with my mom at night, leaving her boyfriend home with us. One day, my cousin's boyfriend came into my room and took me out of my bed. Some of my siblings were at home asleep while others of them were out. He started feeling on me. I was so scared. I told him to stop but he didn't. Then it happened. He took my innocence away.

I'll never forget the first time it happened. That day my life stopped. The little girl who loved playing rope and playing with her dolls and her toys ceased to be. I stopped growing. I stopped dreaming. I went to bed crying every night after it happened. I was so lost. No one saw me crying out. No one saw me hurting.

After that first time, he would come in my room every night to get me. I started going to get in my mom's bed to wait for her to come home so she could protect me. But she never came. Every night, he would come into her room and get me and do whatever he wanted to do to me.

My innocence was taken away and the little girl began to hide. After each time it happened, I felt like I was going to die inside. Feeling worthless and scared, I thought it was all my fault. My mind began to race, and I thought my heart was going to jump out of my chest each night as I walked to my room. I would lay on my bed as tears began to flow down my face. I felt confused. I would ask myself, *"Is this how life should be?"* and say to myself, *"I don't understand."*

I was so afraid to go to sleep at night. Every night I would dream that my cousin's boyfriend was coming for me. There were days when I didn't want the nighttime to come because I was so afraid. I would always want it to be morning, yet my life was filled with such darkness.

I was afraid of every man that came my way. I became fearful that they would hurt me too.

I never told anyone what I was going through at home. I began to act out and have a bad attitude. I hated who I was. I was angry at myself, as well as with my mother and my father. I felt like no one was there to protect me when they should have been. I started getting in trouble at school and was often suspended. I began picking fights with other kids hoping that someone would notice me. But no one was paying attention to me. I would stay in my room trying to hide away. We were left home alone all the time with "that man" (my cousin's boyfriend). I remember saying to myself, *"The wounds and scars that I have inside will never heal."*

I would always wonder, *"Will this pain ever go away?"*

I would never want a child to feel the pain I felt growing up when my innocence was taken away from me. I felt rejected, lonely, and broken.

There is a poem that I wrote that I'd like to share called "The Little Girl That Hides Inside of Me." The poem speaks of how I felt all the years that I was being abused and neglected by people who were supposed to take care of me. It speaks of the life of a lost, scared, and lonely little girl.

The Little Girl That Hides Inside of Me

The little girl that hides inside of me.
Wants her mom but she's never there.
The little girl that hides inside of me
wants a hug and wants to be loved.
The little girl that hides inside of me
is afraid because the boogieman
comes in her room every night to get her.
The little girl that hides inside of me
cries and cries herself to sleep every night
because of the pain she feels deep inside.
The little girl that hides inside of me
wonders will she ever be the woman
God wants her to be.
Now that she's grown,
the little girl that hides inside still peeks out.
The little girl that hides inside
of the young woman.

CHAPTER 2

The Child Within

There is an "inner younger part" in a lot of us that has not had the opportunity to be heard in a positive healthy way. The cry we hear from deep in our hearts comes from the wounded stuck child within. Many of us have experienced trauma in our lives; and to protect and defend ourselves from future sufferings, we often try to forget those painful times we have had in life. This is what I tried to do.

Soon after my cousin's boyfriend started abusing me, my mom had me and my little brother move in with my aunt. That's when things went from bad...to worse.

My first thought was, *"Yes, I'm moving out of my house to a house where I'll be safe from my molester."* But I was wrong, and soon found out it was like living in HELL…or at least what I would imagine HELL to be like.

My aunt treated us like we were her enemies and slaves. She never even let us sit at her table to eat. We had to sit on the floor as well as sleep on the floor. We weren't allowed to sit on her living room chairs. We never went to bed at a decent time. She would go to Bingo which let out at 10 pm. Since we weren't allowed to go to sleep until she got home, we would end up having to stay up until 11 or 12 at night. If we told my aunt that we were tired, we would get beaten or slapped.

Can you imagine being hungry and tired and scared at a young age and not being able to tell anyone including your guardian?

My aunt would make me and my brother mash her leg for hours straight, because it hurt her, and she had issues with it. She worked at a place called Rainbow Hotel. This place was a nightmare! There were constantly prostitutes and crack heads in and out of the hotel. She would make us clean all the rooms. We saw crack bottles and needles at the age of 9 and 10. We were scared at night to go in to clean the rooms. If the rooms weren't cleaned the way she wanted them cleaned, we would get yelled at. We would leave the hotel at about 4:00 in the morning every day, but we still had to get up at 7 am to go to school. We would be so tired.

My aunt used to make my brother and I get on our knees and smack each other in the face. It would hurt so badly. She would say, "Harder! Harder!"

If we didn't hit hard, she would hit us. I remember her putting cigarettes in an ashtray and making us smoke them. She would take the seasoning out of the cabinet and mix it with eggs and make us drink it for no reason. Just because she felt like it.

I remember her making my brother sit in the snow completely naked and then beating him with a knife for wetting himself. I used to run away from home. I was very, very afraid.

I hated my life because we were so mistreated. We weren't nurtured, loved, or free to just be "children."

CHAPTER 3

Thirsty

As I got older, I became promiscuous. I started looking for love in the wrong places. I began going from man to man having sex with them thinking, *"This is love,"* and *"Oh, they love me,"* not realizing that it really wasn't love at all and that they just wanted my body, not my heart. I kept waking up feeling the same way – lost, hurt, confused, and lonely. I was searching for love and had a void in my life that needed to be filled. Although I was looking for love, I just couldn't seem to find it. I was empty and just wanted someone to love me, hold me, and hug me. I was looking for the attention I so desperately needed from when I was younger but never got.

I remember one day that I was going through so much. I didn't understand why I was doing some of the things that I was doing, and I wanted to take my life. I cried and cried because I was hurting. I wanted out of this life. I wanted to stop sleeping around, but I didn't know how.

I said to myself, *"This can't be how I'm going to keep living my life. I have to do better for myself."*

Every time I felt down or got disappointed or got let down, I would run to men. Yes, I was in church every week, but I was going in empty and leaving out empty. I would cry out to God every time I would sleep with a man saying, "I am sorry God. Forgive me Lord. I don't know how to stop."

I was tired, so tired of going back and forth. I felt like the woman at the well. I needed God. Jesus told the women, "Come drink from this water, and you will thirst no more."

Now I know that no man can fulfill the love I was looking for…only God can. My body is the temple of God. I had to learn the benefits of intimacy with my Heavenly Father. God wants intimacy with me. He wants my love relationship, closeness, one on one time, compassion, and passion.

The greatest commandment is, "Love the Lord God with all your heart, mind, and soul." The new commandment is, "Love your neighbor as yourself."

I needed to give God my heart. God knows how close or far I am. By reading the Word I learned that God and the Word are one. I have to stand on the Word so my life can get better. When I stay in God's Word, I am staying close with God and walking with God. If I reject the Word, then I reject God. If you're not in love with the Word, then you are not in love with God. I've come to learn this down through the years through building my relationship with God and studying His Word. God began to quench my thirst. He is the only one who ever could.

.

CHAPTER 4

Broken For Freedom

I wanted to start a new chapter in my life, so I moved out of Paterson to start over. I was still in darkness. I used to dream every night about me being in the dark trying to find my way out. In those dreams, I was running and running but could never seem to find my way out. I was lost. It was hard for me to sleep at night. The devil had me bound. He had me thinking that my life could not change and that I would be broken and messed up for the rest of my life.

When I moved to my new place, I met a lady, and we became close friends. However, it turns out that what I thought was friendship really wasn't. We started doing Black Magic. During this time, I thought that everything was good and that I was going to get better. Because I was looking and searching for someone to be there for me, I was fooled into thinking I was on the right track. Instead, I ended up taking anything that came my way that looked good. But it actually wasn't.

The lady had a class every night for three weeks on Black Magic. She had me light candles in my bedroom, and I had to open my door and let the spirits in my house so they could protect me. I had to put people's pictures on a paper and then write things next to the pictures. I also had to have a rock in my room with flowers.

But I didn't know any better. I thought my life was going to get better, not realizing that by doing these things I was attaching myself to all of these spirits and creating soul ties. I was still lost. I became depressed and stressed out. There were days that I would stay in my room and lay on my bed and just cry and sleep. I wanted to be free, but I didn't know how to get free.

I continued to go to church every Sunday, still leaving out the same way I came in just like I always had, all the time crying out to God. I started to believe that God didn't hear me. I needed God in my life so badly. I was so tired of being tired. I was willing to do any and everything just to make it right with God.

Around this time, I met another friend named Ruby Davis. She would often tell me that she had an aunt and uncle that were pastors. Not knowing that God was setting me up, I kept saying, "Oh okay. I'll go." But I never went. One Sunday in 2012, I finally decided to go. When I did, I met Overseer and Pastor Perry. That's how my life changed. They spoke into and over my life. They began to show me the love of God. They began to tell me that I have a purpose and destiny in life. At first, I didn't really understand what it all meant, but I kept going until I received revelation and began to understand. As time went by, I became a member of that church and started moving in the right direction. I realized that I had to be broken in order to get to freedom. God wanted to set me free. God wanted to be my first love. I began to talk to God and build a relationship with Him. I used to say, "I messed up. I let you down so many times. How can you forgive me?"

I heard God say He would "never leave me or forsake me." He was with me all the time. He let me know that He forgave me for my sins. He would always have open arms for me and always love me no matter how many times I messed up.

Now I can stand and say I am free. I have my freedom. I have my new life that God gave me.

God changed me. He made me the person that I am this day, and I don't look like what I've been through!

Galatians 5:22-26 says, "But the fruit of the Spirit is love, joy, peace, forbearance, kindness, goodness, faithfulness, gentleness, and self-control. Against such things there is no law. Those who belong to Christ Jesus have crucified the flesh with its passions and desire. Since we live by the Spirit, let us keep in step with the Spirit. Let us not become conceited, provoking and envying each other."

God's Word and Spirit have changed my life.

Now I can walk in my new SHAPE in God.

S – Spiritual gifts
H – Heart
A – Ability
P – Personality
E – Experience

Spiritual Gifts

wisdom, knowledge, faith, healing, working of miracles, prophecy.

Heart

Whatever has your heart will have you. It has you. What is in your heart, there your treasure will be. Use your old past as a testimony. Put your feet on the devil, and share your testimony with someone to bring deliverance and healing to them.

Abilities

Estimate your ability. How valuable is it? What are you good at? Know your strengths and weaknesses. Stay committed to God. Sometimes God will use situations to bring up to surface those things that are hidden or set aside that need to be removed.

Personality

Your personality makes you unique. Never allow someone to build a relationship with you based on a flesh level rather than a spiritual level.

Experiences

You have been shaped from experiences. Many have been out of your control. God has used your experiences to shape you into your *new* shape.

I have grown so much in my life. I've come a long way. I thank Overseer (now Apostle) Perry and Pastor (Prophetess) Perry for believing in me and helping me to get to where I am now. They helped me to see that I have a purpose in my life and God is taking me to a new place in Him. Now I am walking in my new identity according to 2 Corinthians 5:17, Philippians 4;13, and Romans 8:37.

CHAPTER 5

Born For Greatness

I am born for greatness. God wants me to see myself as He sees me. I am chosen. I am special. After having my heart and trust broken so many times in life, I have learned that it's okay to be angry, sad, hurt, and disappointed...but to allow God into the process. I don't stay in that place or give room for the enemy to invite himself in.

I don't apologize anymore for expressing my feelings. Instead, I put them at the throne of grace and let God do His healing and restorative work in my life.

Some people are led by their feelings. Everything they do in life is motivated by what they feel. When they are up, everyone knows, and when they are down...everyone knows! I urge you... don't be a lukewarm Christian. Don't allow yourself to be led by your emotions.

This is the way that I used to be. Fight your feelings. Don't look for God in how you feel. You will miss Him. Stabilize your mind through the Word. It's in the Word where you will find your joy, peace, love, and strength. It's in the Word of God that you will find your purpose. In the Word, you will find and realize that you were born for greatness.

Don't let anybody take that away from you. Don't let what happened to you in your past take that away from you. Don't let the enemy take that away. His job is to steal, kill, and destroy, but Jesus came so that you can live and live the abundant life that God has for you. Always remember that no matter what happens to you, you were born for greatness!

CHAPTER 6

What Is Trust?

I had to learn what "trust" was because for so long I couldn't trust anyone. Trust is – firm belief in the reliability of someone or something. Relationships have to be built on trust, defined also as: confidence, belief, faith, certainty, assurance, conviction, credence, and reliance.

The bottom line is good relationships are built on trust. I remember a time when I had trust issues. I had difficulty trusting anyone, especially men. Everyone I let into my life, I ended up pushing away because I would think, *"They are going to hurt me too."* It was too hard for me to trust. I couldn't even trust my leaders at that point in my life. I thought, *"They're going to hurt me like the others did."*

I remember when I first came to the ministry. Pastor looked me in my eyes as tears began to fall down my face and said to me, "We (Overseer and Pastor) are not going to abandon you. We are not going to hurt you. We are not going to leave you."

It was so hard for me to believe her. I didn't know how to receive the love and honesty that they gave me.

As the years went by, I began to watch and listen to my pastors and see the love of God in them. They taught the Word. They preached the Word. They lived the Word. It was God, God's Word, Word all day and every day in their lives. They taught me how to trust myself, and they let me know that I could trust them in my life. God lived in them. He sent them into my life. I learned that trust covers a whole lot of things. When I started to trust, my life changed, and it came with a newness. It came with healing. I began to walk in the ways of God. I had to see myself being a trophy of my past. Overseer once told me, "Don't trust God or the Word with your emotions, because you will never grow in God."

That stuck with me, and I began to trust God in the Holy Spirit. Proverbs 3:5-7 says, "Trust in the Lord with all your heart and lean not on your own understanding. In all your ways acknowledge him and he will make your paths straight."

If you want a relationship with God, you have to believe that Jesus took the pain on the cross to give you a new life. We have to learn to trust God in every circumstance. Psalm 91:2 reads, "I will say of the Lord, He is my refuge and my fortress my God in Him will I trust."

I believe that faith and trust go hand in hand. They are like a one-two punch. First, you must have faith that God exists and that He is who the Bible says He is, and then you have to trust that God can and will change your life around. I used to depend on people. I had to ask God to deliver me from people, because in important times of my life, people were my source. That's not the way it's supposed to be. God is my source. People are my resource. You have to have a relationship with God in order for you to trust Him. Now I know who I am. I know who I was created to be. I used to think that my life didn't matter. I used to feel that no one cared. Have you ever been in a room with so many people but still feel that you're in there all alone? I always felt left out and that whatever I did didn't matter. God let me see that my life does matter, that I have a purpose and a destiny. I had to learn that.

Psalm 37:4 tells us to "Delight thyself also in the Lord and He shall give thee the desires of thine heart."

Don't delight yourself in people or in things. You will confuse the enemy when you delight yourself in the Lord. Jesus is the real thing. I learned in life that Jesus is the only one that can fulfill me and give me the desires of my heart. A changed mind is a changed life. I thank God for His hand that He has over my life. I owe God a praise. When I look back and think about how far I have come and where God brought me from, I thank God for having His hands on my life because I could have been dead and gone. I owe God everything. I would never have known that I have a destiny and purpose in life if it wasn't for God's hand on me. I would have lost my mind, went astray or given up but God's hand held me and kept me. If it had not been for God's hand on my life, I wouldn't have known His plan.

As I sit here and think about how far God has brought me and how far I have come in my life, I'm so thankful. Even though my dad is not here, I forgive him for not being there for me. I have a good relationship with some of my family, and even though it's still a work in progress, God has given me the grace and compassion to work on my relationship with my mom. I've learned through the years that you only get one mom. Although God has given me many spiritual moms which I am thankful for, there is only one mother that birthed me, and I've learned that I should love her no matter what. I was able to get past my anger towards her and I love her with all my heart.

I learned in the years of building my relationship with God that I can't close my heart nor lose patience while waiting on the Lord. He is faithful in all things including His timing in perfecting my issues. Through trusting God, I now know what trust is. I have peace in knowing that I can put and keep my trust in God!

CHAPTER 7

The Power of God Makes Us Free

This prayer is for you. Say this prayer out loud:

Father God, I humbly come to you today giving you all that I am. Thank you for fulfilling every desire in my heart. Mold me and shape me into your image. Remove anything from my life that is displeasing to you so that everything I am brings glory to you. Amen.

You know we all have weaknesses. No one wants to be weak. It makes them feel that they're not strong and not capable of doing anything, but spiritually your weakness can be used by God. Don't let the enemy undermine the call that God has on your life because of some area of weakness that you have. The enemy created dry and wasted places early in your life. He thought that by attacking your innocence and your identity, he would make it impossible for you to trust God. Your pain and scars were planned by the enemy so you wouldn't trust God. The enemy wants you to see yourself in the eyes of your pain and your scars, but God wants to use your weakness. Don't let the devil discourage you and tell you your weakness is a problem. Know that your weakness can help you grow in God if you give that weakness to Him. Remember that Proverbs 3:5 says to "Trust in the Lord with all thine heart and lean not unto thine own understanding 3:6 in all thy ways, acknowledge him and he shall direct your paths."

My childhood was hard. As I got older, I had to realize that even though I went through a lot of things in my youth, through them, God was preparing me to minister to young girls and women that have gone through what I went through. God was going to use me to speak to them about how to get out of it, and to encourage them not to let their past determine their future.

Now I have a heart for young people. The love that I have for kids is powerful. When I see them hurting or going through things, I step right in to help them because my heart goes out to every child that hurts. My heart goes out to that child that never talks about what they are going through, that child that's afraid to go to sleep at night, that child that can't talk to their mom, that child that has a silent cry, and that child that stopped growing and thinks their life is over and that they will never be anything in life.

Know that God doesn't make mistakes. You are not a mistake. You should see yourself how God sees you. God sees you as beautiful. You are beautiful in God's eyes. Look in the mirror of God and see how beautiful you are.

Romans 8:28 says, "And I know that all things work together for good to those who love God to those who are called according to His purpose."

Always remember that God has a plan for your life. I learned that we have to be Kingdom minded people. We have to protect the seed (children). We must continually intercede and speak the Word over and to our children, especially when the enemy comes...and he will come.

We must rebuke and expose Satan and his tactics for the sake of our children. We have to keep the character, integrity, and standard so there will be no more little girls and little boys living inside of the woman or the man. God wants to heal you totally so you can be free and so you can be whole.

The little girl that lives inside of me is okay now. She has been set free from her pain and insecurities. I thank God for healing her and making her whole. I thank God that I am free!

ABOUT THE AUTHOR

Cynthia V. Avent was born and raised in Paterson New Jersey. She attended and graduated from Silk City Academy in 2004. She is a member of Hallelujah Christian Fellowship Church located in Union, NJ where Bishop Eddie Bennett is pastor and Dr. Yvonne Bennett is Co-pastor.

Cynthia loves helping others and being a role model. She has mentored many girls in her life. She was inspired to write a book to help a lot of people that have gone through the same thing that she's gone through in life. She is a strong believer in Jesus Christ, her Lord and Savior. Cynthia has served as an usher, sung in the choir, and ministered through her gift of praise dancing. She is a liturgical dance instructor. She has been an instructor for many step teams and participated in many plays: "Black-On-Black Crime" on 07/12/2007, "A Woman's Temple" on 07/12/2008, which she was the main character, "Hip-Hop Spelling Bee" on 07/09/2009, and "A Father's Repentance" on 06/12/2010.

She was a cheerleader coach, where she worked with the youth and also had a youth group (which specialized in taking the youth off the streets). She received her certificate of CDA (Child Development Associate) in 2016. She was blessed to adopt her sister's three children.

ORDER INFORMATION

You can order additional copies of *The Little Girl That Hides of Me* as indicated below:

Books are available at Amazon.com, Kindle and Your Local Bookstores (By Request)

Please leave a review for this book on Amazon and let other readers know how much you enjoyed reading it.

Thank you!

Made in the USA
Middletown, DE
15 September 2021